Goldie the Owl and the Golden Treasure: Simple Lessons on Gold

Dedication

To my three beautiful daughters, Giulia, Giorgia, and Nicole—

This book is for you.

May you always follow your curiosity, seek wisdom in everything you do, and remember that the greatest treasures in life are the lessons we share and the love we give.

With all my heart,

Daddy

Preface

As I began writing this book, my goal was clear: I wanted to introduce children to the unique qualities of gold—not just as a shiny object but as a symbol of stability, patience, and value. From my experience, I've seen how important it is to understand these concepts early, and I believe that just like learning about saving and sharing, learning about gold can be both fun and valuable for kids.

The idea for this book was inspired by several stories that I hold dear. *The Gruffalo* had always struck me as a brilliant way to draw young readers into a world of imagination, filled with lessons wrapped in adventure. I wanted to achieve something similar, to make kids eager to explore the Golden Forest and meet its characters. At the same time, I looked to *Who Moved My Cheese?* which has a way of teaching simple but powerful lessons through relatable events. Every chapter here follows that same principle—each adventure with Goldie leads to a clear message about gold and its role in life.

I also wanted the story to be rich in detail, which is why I took inspiration from John Steinbeck's style. I wanted to create vivid, descriptive scenes that children could visualise while introducing new vocabulary to help them expand their understanding of the world around them. Every word was chosen to both entertain and educate.

Goldie, the wise little owl, represents the curiosity we all have when we're young. Her journey through the Golden Forest is more than just a story—it's a way to teach children about the value of saving, patience, and trust. I hope this book helps spark conversations about these principles at an age where they can truly make a lasting impact.

My hope is that through Goldie's adventures, children will learn more than just the qualities of gold—they'll learn about the importance of thinking ahead, making wise decisions, and understanding what truly holds value.

Dr Alessio Faccia

Introduction

The Golden Forest was not like any other place you could imagine. Nestled deep between rolling hills and sparkling rivers, the trees there shimmered faintly, not because of sunlight or morning dew, but because hidden amongst their roots and branches lay little specks of gold. The forest was alive with the sounds of creatures, each busily going about their day, but the air felt calm, as though the trees themselves were keeping a secret.

In this forest, the creatures didn't fight over food or water. No, what they treasured most were the tiny golden nuggets they sometimes found scattered underfoot. These weren't just ordinary shiny things but treasures of such importance that even the oldest creatures couldn't fully explain why. Some called them the forest's wisdom, while others simply called them gold.

It was here that Goldie lived, high up in the hollow of an ancient oak. Goldie was unlike the other owls. While most were content to hunt at night and sleep by day, Goldie's bright yellow eyes stayed open to the world, always looking, always wondering. There was something about the Golden Forest that she couldn't quite put her talon on, something more than just the rustling leaves or the singing breeze.

Goldie had seen the other animals scurrying about, collecting gold with great care. Penny the Squirrel had stuffed her nest with shiny nuggets, even more than her acorns. Turtle Tim, slow but sure, moved between the streams, always on the lookout for a golden glint in the mud. Even the clever Foxy Fred had an eye for these golden pieces, though his interest seemed more in the thrill of the chase than in what he did with them afterwards.

But Goldie? Goldie was curious. Why did everyone in the Golden Forest want these bits of gold? They couldn't eat them, they couldn't wear them, and they didn't keep anyone warm at night. Yet still, day after day, the forest creatures worked for them, storing them away like treasures of immeasurable value. The mystery gnawed at Goldie, and soon, she decided there was only one way to find out.

With a quiet flutter of wings and a mind full of questions, Goldie set off on a journey through the Golden Forest. She would speak to the other creatures, watch them, learn from them, and perhaps discover the truth about these golden nuggets. Little did she know, what she was about to learn wasn't just about the gold itself but about something much more important: why some things, even if they don't seem to have a use right away, are worth keeping safe.

As Goldie's yellow eyes sparkled with wonder, she felt it—this was the start of something big. And so, with the soft rustle of leaves and the quiet hum of the forest around her, Goldie's adventure began.

Chapter 1: Goldie's Curiosity

It was a warm, quiet morning in the Golden Forest. The sun hadn't quite risen yet, and a soft mist clung to the ground like a blanket. Goldie, wide awake as always, perched on the branch of her favourite tree. Below her, she spotted Penny the Squirrel, busily collecting something shiny. Not acorns, as Goldie expected, but small golden nuggets.

Penny's tail flicked from side to side as she tucked the nuggets away in a hollowed-out part of the tree trunk. She worked quickly, with great care, as though each piece was more precious than the last. Goldie tilted her head, confused. "Why isn't she gathering acorns? Winter will be here soon," Goldie thought to herself. Acorns were food, and food meant survival. But these golden nuggets? What good were they?

Curiosity fluttered in her chest, and before she knew it, Goldie swooped down to meet Penny.

"Good morning, Penny!" Goldie hooted softly, landing on a low branch. "I've been watching you. You're gathering all these shiny things instead of acorns. Aren't you worried about food for the winter?"

Penny paused, glancing up at Goldie with a quick smile. "Oh, I've got plenty of acorns hidden away," she said, brushing off the question. "But these," she added, holding up one of the golden nuggets, "these are even more important."

Goldie blinked, confused. "But you can't eat them. Why are they more important?"

Penny sat back on her haunches, looking thoughtfully at the little piece of gold in her paw. "It's true, Goldie, I can't eat them. But these golden nuggets will keep me safe. Acorns come and go; sometimes, there are lots, and sometimes there are none. But gold? It never loses its shine. It's always worth something, even when the acorns run out."

Goldie ruffled her feathers. "But how can something that doesn't fill your belly be so important?"

Penny stood up, tucking the nugget away in her stash. "Gold isn't for eating, no, but it's for protecting what you have. When the time comes, and everything around is scarce, these nuggets will hold their value. They're a shield when other things fail."

Goldie watched as Penny scampered off, her head buzzing with thoughts. It didn't make sense yet, but she could feel a lesson stirring. She perched back on her branch, deep in thought.

As the sun rose higher in the sky, Goldie thought about what she had seen. Acorns were food, yes. But they could spoil, or be eaten by someone else. Gold didn't spoil, and no matter what happened in the forest, it would always stay valuable. Even though it didn't give Penny food right now, it was something she could rely on when times got tough.

And then, like the sun breaking through the mist, the lesson became clear: Some things, even if they don't seem important today, are worth saving for tomorrow.

Goldie's yellow eyes gleamed with understanding. She had learned her first lesson in the Golden Forest. Not all treasures are meant to be eaten or used right away—some are meant to protect what you have when you need it most.

With a gentle flap of her wings, Goldie flew back to her nest, ready for the next day's questions. She was starting to understand why everyone in the forest cared so much about gold. It wasn't just about what it could do today, but what it would mean for the future.

Chapter 2: Meeting Banker Bear

The next morning, Goldie awoke with the first rays of sunlight, her mind still swirling with thoughts of Penny and the golden nuggets. Determined to understand more, she set off through the Golden Forest. As she glided through the crisp morning air, she saw him—Banker Bear, sitting under the shade of an enormous oak tree. He was known to be wise and patient, always sitting by his tree, offering advice to any creature who asked. Today, Goldie had questions of her own.

Landing softly on a branch near him, Goldie called out, "Good morning, Banker Bear! May I ask you something?"

Banker Bear looked up from the pile of acorns he had been sorting, his large brown eyes twinkling behind his spectacles. "Of course, young Goldie. What is it you wish to know?"

Goldie hopped closer, her wings fluttering with curiosity. "I spoke to Penny the Squirrel yesterday. She told me that the gold nuggets she collects are more important than acorns because they keep her safe when times get tough. But I still don't quite understand how something you can't eat could be so important. Can you explain?"

Banker Bear smiled kindly and gestured for Goldie to come closer. "You see, Goldie," he began, "acorns, just like food or anything else that is useful, can come and go. You might have many acorns one year and very few the next. But gold? Gold never spoils, and it never changes. It keeps its value no matter what happens."

Goldie tilted her head. "But if you can't eat it, how does it help?"

Banker Bear chuckled softly, his belly shaking. "It helps differently. Think of it like this: the forest has seasons. Some seasons are full of food, while others are harsh and dry. During those harsh times, gold was like a promise that held its worth. You can trade it for what you need, and you know it will always be valuable, no matter how bad things get."

Goldie's feathers ruffled with a new question. "But why not just save more acorns or berries?"

Banker Bear reached for one of the golden nuggets resting beside him. "Because acorns and berries can go bad, or other creatures might take them. But gold? It's rare, and it doesn't disappear. It's like this old oak tree. Its roots are deep and strong, weathering every storm. It may not give fruit every season, but it stands tall, offering its strength when the winds howl."

Goldie's eyes widened. "So, gold is like an anchor in a storm?"

"Exactly," Banker Bear nodded. "When the world around you becomes uncertain, gold is the one thing you can trust to remain strong. That's why we treasure it."

Goldie felt the weight of Banker Bear's words. She had always thought of wealth in terms of food and shelter, things that provided for the moment. But now, she began to understand that gold was about something more—a safety net for when life became uncertain.

As Goldie prepared to take flight, she paused and looked back at Banker Bear. "So, it's not just about having gold. It's about knowing that when times get tough, you'll have something strong to rely on?"

Banker Bear smiled warmly. "You've got it, Goldie. Gold may not feed you today, but it will protect you tomorrow."

As Goldie soared through the treetops, the lesson settled in her heart: When the winds of change blow, it's good to have something solid to hold onto.

Goldie felt wiser now. The Golden Forest was full of lessons, and she was ready to learn them all. Today, she had discovered that gold wasn't just a treasure—it was security in an uncertain world.

Chapter 3: The Lesson of Turtle Tim

The days in the Golden Forest rolled by, each one bringing Goldie closer to understanding the mystery of gold. She had learned from Penny that gold was something you kept for the future and from Banker Bear that it was like a strong tree in a storm, holding its value no matter what. But there was still something nagging at the back of her mind. If gold was so important, why wasn't everyone rushing around to gather as much as they could?

One afternoon, while soaring low over the forest floor, Goldie spotted a familiar, slow-moving figure plodding along the edge of the stream—Turtle Tim. He was one of the oldest creatures in the forest, known for his steady pace and quiet wisdom. Unlike the other animals, Tim never seemed to be in a hurry, yet he always got to where he needed to be. Goldie felt a flutter of curiosity and swooped down to join him.

"Good afternoon, Tim!" she called, landing gracefully beside him.

Turtle Tim, his wrinkled face breaking into a slow smile, nodded. "Afternoon, Goldie," he said in his low, steady voice. "What brings you here, my young friend?"

Goldie walked alongside him, her feathers ruffling in the soft breeze. "I've been learning about gold," she began, "and everyone says it's so important because it keeps its value and protects us when times get tough. But I don't understand why you're not in a hurry to collect more of it. Shouldn't we be racing to gather as much as we can?"

Tim chuckled—a slow, deep sound that rumbled like distant thunder. "Ah, Goldie, not everything in life is a race. Sometimes, it's better to be steady than to be fast. Let me show you something."

Goldie followed Tim to the edge of the stream, where the water flowed gently over smooth rocks. Tim lowered his head and pointed to a single golden nugget sitting quietly at the bottom of the streambed. It wasn't shiny like the nuggets Penny collected, but it was there, waiting.

"See that nugget?" Tim asked, his eyes twinkling. "It's been sitting there for who knows how long. The stream flows over it, the seasons change, but it stays right where it is. It doesn't lose its value just because it's sitting there quietly."

Goldie stared at the nugget, puzzled. "But it's not doing anything."

"Exactly," Tim said with a nod. "Gold doesn't need to do anything to hold its value. It doesn't rush around or change with the seasons like the leaves on the trees. It's patient, just like I am. And because of that, it will always be there when you need it, no matter how much time has passed."

Goldie perched on a nearby rock, thinking. "So, it's not about how quickly you collect it, but that it's there when you need it?"

Tim smiled again, his wrinkled face full of warmth. "That's right, young one. Gold teaches us that sometimes, slow and steady wins the race. It doesn't spoil, it doesn't rush, and it doesn't change with the wind. It waits. And when the time is right, it's there to protect you."

Goldie's feathers rustled with understanding. She had been thinking about gold the wrong way. It wasn't about gathering it quickly or using it right away. It was about knowing that, like Turtle Tim, it would always be there, moving at its own pace, ready when you needed it most.

As the sun dipped lower in the sky, casting a golden glow over the forest, Goldie spread her wings and prepared to take off. But before she left, she turned to Tim and asked, "So the lesson is to be patient with gold? That it's not about how fast you get it, but about trusting that it will be there when the time comes?"

Tim nodded slowly. "Exactly, Goldie. Gold, like all good things, rewards patience. It doesn't rush, and neither should you."

As Goldie flew back toward her nest, the quiet of the forest settling around her, she felt a deep sense of peace. Today, she had learned that gold was more than just a shiny treasure—it was a lesson in patience, in trusting that sometimes the best things come to those who wait.

And as she nestled into her tree for the night, Goldie remembered the day's lesson: True value doesn't rush. It waits patiently until the time is right.

Goldie knew there were still more lessons to come, but tonight, she had learned the value of patience, and that was enough.

Chapter 4: Foxy Fred's Shortcut

The morning light filtered through the dense trees of the Golden Forest as Goldie stretched her wings and prepared for another day of discovery. She had learned so much already—from Penny's caution with gold to Turtle Tim's lesson in patience. But Goldie had a feeling that there was still more to understand.

As she flew over the forest, her keen eyes spotted Foxy Fred, sly as ever, darting in and out of the bushes near the riverbank. Fred was known for his cleverness and quick thinking, always looking for the next big thing that would get him ahead. Goldie, curious as always, decided to follow him for a while.

Foxy Fred seemed to be up to something. He wasn't hunting or playing his usual tricks on the other animals. No, today Fred was gathering gold—piles of it—much faster than anyone else in the forest. His quick paws scooped up shiny nuggets from the ground, stashing them into a large, makeshift pouch. It didn't take long before Fred noticed Goldie watching him from a nearby branch.

"Well, well, Goldie! Fancy seeing you here!" Fred called, grinning mischievously. "What brings you to my little corner of the forest?"

Goldie tilted her head. "I've been learning about gold. Everyone says it's important to save it for when times get tough. But you're gathering so much, so quickly. Why are you in such a hurry?"

Fred's grin widened. "Ah, Goldie, that's because I'm smarter than the others! While they're busy taking their time and being careful, I'm getting ahead. Why wait for gold to protect you later when you can use it to get ahead right now?"

Goldie blinked in surprise. "What do you mean?"

Fred leaned in closer, his voice lowering to a conspiratorial whisper. "You see, I've found a shortcut. I'm going to take all this gold and trade it for something even better. There's a market down by the big oak tree. If I trade quickly, I can turn this gold into something that'll give me even more. Forget waiting around for it to protect me later! I'll be rich today."

Goldie's feathers ruffled with uncertainty. Something didn't feel quite right. "But what if it doesn't work? What if you lose the gold in a bad trade?"

Fred waved his paw dismissively. "Nonsense! I'm too clever for that. Why wait until you have everything now? Patience is for turtles and squirrels. Foxes like me are quick and smart."

Without waiting for a response, Fred bounded off, his pouch of gold clinking as he disappeared into the trees. Goldie watched him go, her heart heavy with doubt. Something about Fred's plan seemed risky. He was rushing, and rushing wasn't something she had learned from the others.

As the day went on, Goldie flew around the forest, thinking about what Fred had said. Maybe there was something to his idea. Maybe quick thinking and fast trades were the way to get ahead. But the more she thought about it, the more unsure she felt.

It wasn't until late afternoon that Goldie spotted Fred again. This time, though, he wasn't grinning. He was slumped near the stream, his pouch empty and his head hanging low.

"Fred!" Goldie called, swooping down beside him. "What happened?"

Fred sighed, his cleverness gone. "I made a bad trade, Goldie. I was so sure I could turn all my gold into something better, but it didn't work out. Now it's all gone."

Goldie sat beside him quietly. She didn't say, "I told you so," even though part of her wanted to. Instead, she offered a gentle hoot of sympathy. "I'm sorry, Fred."

Fred looked at her, his usual spark dimmed. "I should've listened to you and maybe to the others. I rushed. I wanted to get rich quick, but now I have nothing."

Goldie thought about what Banker Bear and Turtle Tim had taught her. She knew Fred was feeling down, but maybe this was a lesson he needed to learn. She ruffled her feathers and spoke softly. "It's okay, Fred. We all make mistakes. But I think there's something you can learn from this."

Fred raised an eyebrow. "What's that?"

Goldie smiled kindly. "Gold isn't about quick wins or shortcuts. It's about protecting what you have. Sometimes, it's better to be slow and steady, like Tim. Rushing may feel exciting, but it can also lead to losing everything. Gold is valuable because it lasts, not because it's fast."

Fred nodded slowly, his clever grin replaced with a more thoughtful expression. "You're right, Goldie. I guess I got carried away."

As Goldie prepared to fly back to her nest, she looked at Fred one more time and said, "The lesson here is simple: If you rush to riches, you might end up with nothing. But if you're careful and patient, your gold will protect you for a long time."

Fred nodded in agreement, and with a sigh, he stood up, ready to start fresh. Goldie took off into the sky, feeling proud of the lesson she had shared. She had learned something important today—not just about gold, but about the dangers of rushing through life. Gold, like many things, needed time and care. And that was a lesson worth remembering.

Chapter 5: Goldie's Realisation

The days in the Golden Forest passed as quietly as ever, with each creature going about its business. Goldie had spent weeks learning from her forest friends about gold—how it protected, how it rewarded patience, and how rushing could lead to trouble. But despite all she had learned, there was still one question that lingered in her mind: Why was gold, of all things, so important? She had gathered the lessons, but she wanted to understand the deeper reason why gold was such a treasured thing.

One misty morning, Goldie perched on a high branch, gazing over the Golden Forest. From her vantage point, she could see all the creatures moving below—Penny gathering acorns and gold nuggets, Turtle Tim slowly making his way along the stream, and even Foxy Fred, who had slowed down since his mishap. Each of them valued gold, but for different reasons. Goldie realised she was missing something, a final piece to the puzzle.

With a determined flap of her wings, Goldie soared down through the trees, heading toward the centre of the forest, where the Great Oak stood. It was said that this ancient tree had seen all the changes in the forest, from seasons of plenty to times of scarcity. Maybe here, Goldie would find the answer she was searching for.

As she arrived at the base of the Great Oak, she found Banker Bear sitting quietly under its wide branches. He was staring at a small pile of gold nuggets in his paw, deep in thought.

"Banker Bear," Goldie called softly, landing next to him, "I've learned a lot about gold from you and the others, but there's still something I don't understand. Why is gold, out of everything, so important to everyone?"

Banker Bear looked up slowly, his eyes twinkling with the wisdom of many seasons. "Ah, Goldie. I wondered when you would come to this question." He patted the ground next to him, and Goldie settled in. "Let me ask you something first—what have you learned so far about gold?"

Goldie thought for a moment before answering. "I've learned that gold protects what we have when times are tough. It holds its value, and unlike acorns or berries, it doesn't spoil or disappear. I've also learned that it rewards patience and that rushing to get more of it can be dangerous, like when Fred lost everything."

Banker Bear nodded, pleased with her understanding. "Yes, you've learned well, Goldie. But do you know why that is? Why gold doesn't spoil or lose its value?"

Goldie tilted her head, puzzled. "No... why?"

"Because," Banker Bear began, holding up one of the gold nuggets, "gold is special. It's rare, and it cannot be made or taken away. It's like the forest itself—no matter what happens around it, gold remains. It doesn't grow or change, and that makes it different from anything else."

Goldie blinked. "So that's why everyone in the forest treasures it so much?"

Banker Bear smiled. "Exactly. When times are good, we don't think much about it. We gather our food, build our homes, and enjoy the sunshine. But when times are hard, when the leaves fall, and the streams dry up, gold is the one thing we can rely on. It can't be destroyed or taken away by time. That's why we collect it—not to spend it quickly, but to hold onto something that lasts."

Goldie felt the truth of his words settles deep in her heart. It wasn't just that gold had value but that it was dependable. In a world where so many things could change—where seasons came and went, and food could run out—gold was constant. It didn't provide food or shelter, but it provided security.

"So the real reason gold is important," Goldie said slowly, "is because it gives us something to hold onto when everything else changes."

Banker Bear nodded again. "Yes, young one. Gold isn't about being rich or having more than others. It's about knowing that no matter what happens, you have something safe. Something solid. That's why the forest treasures it."

Goldie sat quietly for a while, thinking about everything she had learned. She realised now that gold wasn't just about protection or patience. It was about trust—trust that it would be there when everything else was uncertain.

With this new understanding, Goldie smiled. She felt wiser, not just about gold, but about life in the Golden Forest. Every creature had its own way of gathering and saving, but they all shared this one truth: gold was something that stood the test of time, a treasure not because of what it could buy but because of what it could give—security in a world of change.

As she spread her wings to fly home, she thought about what she would remember from this day: Gold is not about riches; it's about having something you can trust when everything else is uncertain.

With that final piece of wisdom tucked away, Goldie soared back into the sky, her heart light and her mind full of the lessons the Golden Forest had taught her. She knew now that gold wasn't just a shiny treasure—it was a promise, a steady presence in a world where nothing else stayed the same. And that was a lesson worth holding onto forever.

Chapter 6: Goldie and the Seasons of Change

The Golden Forest began to shift as autumn arrived. The once bright green leaves turned shades of amber and gold, swirling gently down to the forest floor. Goldie watched the transformation from her perch high in the ancient oak. She had learned so much in the past weeks—about gold, about patience, and about trust. But with the changing seasons came new challenges, and Goldie could feel that her journey was not yet complete.

As the crisp wind rustled the leaves, Goldie noticed something else changing in the forest. The animals, once busy collecting acorns and gold nuggets, were starting to slow down. Penny the

Squirrel seemed more frantic, scurrying around trying to gather the last of the acorns before winter. Turtle Tim was nowhere to be seen, likely preparing to hibernate. Even Foxy Fred, who had learned a valuable lesson about rushing, was cautiously collecting small bits of food to prepare for the colder months.

Goldie, however, felt a calmness in her heart. She had stored away her lessons like the other animals stored their gold. She knew that winter would come and that, with it, there would be difficult times. But Goldie also knew that she was prepared—not with piles of food or hasty plans, but with something more reliable.

One cold morning, as frost sparkled on the ground, Goldie spotted Penny the Squirrel pacing beneath her tree, clearly distressed. Goldie fluttered down to her friend, her wings gently stirring the icy air.

"Penny, what's wrong?" Goldie asked softly.

Penny looked up, her eyes wide with worry. "Oh, Goldie! I've been so busy collecting acorns, but I didn't gather enough! Winter is coming faster than I thought, and I don't have enough food stored away. What if I can't find any more?"

Goldie thought for a moment. "But you've been collecting gold as well, haven't you?"

Penny nodded quickly. "Yes, but gold can't feed me through the winter!"

Goldie smiled gently. "That's true, Penny. But gold is there for times like these. You've been wise to save it. Now, if food becomes scarce, you can trade your gold for what you need. It won't spoil, and it won't disappear. It will protect you, just like it's meant to."

Penny's eyes softened as she considered Goldie's words. "I hadn't thought of it that way. I was so worried about not having enough acorns that I forgot about the gold I'd saved."

Goldie nodded. "That's the thing about gold. It's not for everyday use, but when hard times come, it's there to keep you safe. You've worked hard to gather both food and gold. You'll be okay."

Penny smiled, her tail twitching with relief. "Thank you, Goldie. I feel better now."

As Penny scampered off to check on her stash, Goldie flew back up to her branch, watching as the forest continued to prepare for the colder days ahead. She thought about how each animal approached the change in seasons differently—some with acorns, some with gold, and some with a little of both. The lesson became clear as she observed the balance they all needed to strike.

Later that evening, as the sun dipped low and the forest was bathed in the soft glow of twilight, Goldie felt a new understanding settle within her. The seasons in the forest, much like life, were always changing. Some days were full of abundance, while others brought scarcity. But through it all, the animals that had saved wisely—those who had balanced their needs for both the present and the future—were the ones who would thrive.

And then it came to her: the final lesson of the season. She perched on her branch and whispered it into the wind: Life will always change, but if you prepare wisely, you'll have what you need to weather any storm.

Goldie felt peaceful, knowing that she had learned one of the most important lessons in the Golden Forest. Gold wasn't just about value or trust; it was about balance. It didn't replace food or shelter, but it worked alongside them, protecting the creatures of the forest when times were hard.

As winter crept closer and the days grew shorter, Goldie knew she was ready for whatever came next. She had her own treasures, not of gold, but of wisdom—lessons that would guide her through every season of life. With a final flutter of her wings, she settled into her nest, ready to rest and reflect on the journey that had brought her to this understanding.

Winter was coming, but Goldie wasn't afraid. She had learned that with patience, trust, and balance, she would always have enough to carry her through the changing seasons.

Chapter 7: Goldie's Final Lesson

Winter had fully settled into the Golden Forest. The trees stood bare, their branches stark against the pale sky, and a thick blanket of snow covered the ground. The once bustling forest had quieted as its creatures tucked themselves away, relying on the food and treasures they had saved to see them through the cold months.

Goldie, perched in her nest high up in the ancient oak, looked out over the frosty landscape. She had spent weeks reflecting on all the lessons she had learned about gold, patience, and trust. The forest, though silent, felt full of meaning to her now. She had learned much, but there was one last thing Goldie hadn't fully grasped. What was her own place in all of this? Gold had helped everyone in the forest, but what had she, Goldie the Wise Little Owl, learned about herself?

That morning, with the forest still cloaked in the soft quiet of winter, Goldie decided to pay one last visit to Banker Bear, her old friend and the one who had guided her since the beginning of her journey. She flew through the crisp air, her wings slicing through the mist, and landed at the entrance of Banker Bear's den, nestled at the base of a large pine tree.

"Banker Bear?" she called softly, peeking inside.

A warm, deep voice greeted her. "Come in, Goldie. I've been expecting you."

Goldie entered the den, where Banker Bear sat beside a fire, the soft glow of the flames casting long shadows on the walls. Goldie settled herself near him, her heart calm but full of questions.

"I've learned so much from you and from everyone else in the forest," Goldie began. "I understand now that gold is about patience, trust, and preparing for the future. But there's still something I don't quite understand. What's my place in all this? I've watched everyone else, but what have I truly learned for myself?"

Banker Bear smiled, his old eyes twinkling with warmth. "Ah, young Goldie, the most important lessons are the ones we find within ourselves. You've seen how the creatures of the forest use gold to protect themselves. But have you noticed what you've been doing all along?"

Goldie thought for a moment, unsure. "I've been watching, learning… trying to understand."

Banker Bear nodded. "Yes, but you've been doing something more. Goldie, you've been gathering wisdom just as the others have been gathering gold. You may not have stored up acorns or gold nuggets, but you've collected something just as valuable."

Goldie blinked in surprise. "Wisdom?"

"Yes," Banker Bear said softly. "Every step of your journey, every creature you've met, every lesson you've learned—these have all been treasures, just like gold. But instead of keeping them for yourself, you've shared them with others. You've helped Penny realise the value of her gold when she was worried. You guided Foxy Fred back to the right path when he was lost. You've given more than you've taken, and that, dear Goldie, is a different kind of wealth."

Goldie's feathers fluffed with warmth as she took in his words. She had been so focused on learning about gold that she hadn't realised the true treasure she had been gathering all along: wisdom and the ability to help others.

Banker Bear continued, his voice gentle but full of meaning. "You see, gold protects us during hard times, yes. But wisdom, the kind you've gathered, is something even greater. It's a treasure that grows the more you share it. And that, Goldie, is your place in the Golden Forest. You are the one who helps others see the value in what they have, whether it's gold, patience, or understanding."

Goldie sat quietly for a moment, her heart full. It was as if all the pieces of her journey had finally come together. She had thought that learning about gold would be her greatest lesson, but it was really about what she had given along the way—her guidance, her kindness, her wisdom.

"I understand now," Goldie said softly, her yellow eyes bright with the realisation. "It's not just about collecting treasures for myself. It's about helping others see the value in their own treasures, whether that's gold or something else."

Banker Bear smiled, his face glowing in the firelight. "Exactly, Goldie. You've learned the greatest lesson of all—that the most valuable things in life aren't always the things we can hold in our hands. Sometimes, they're the things we share with others."

As Goldie flew back to her nest that evening, the snow gently falling around her, she felt lighter than ever. She had found her place in the Golden Forest, not as a collector of gold, but as a guide, a helper, a friend. Her wisdom, like the gold that filled the forest, would stand the test of time. And she knew now that no matter what the seasons brought, she was ready.

As she perched in her nest and gazed out over the snow-covered forest, Goldie smiled. She whispered softly to herself the final lesson of her journey: The greatest treasures are not the ones we keep but the ones we share.

And with that, Goldie's heart was full, knowing that she had found something far more precious than gold—a way to help others and a place to call her own in the ever-changing forest.

www.ingramcontent.com/pod-product-compliance
Lightning Source LLC
Chambersburg PA
CBHW030102230526
45471CB00003B/1207